JOINING THE RODEO

RODEO

Tex McLeese

The Rourke Press, Inc.
Vero Beach, Florida 32964

PHOTO CREDITS:
© Dennis K. Clark: title page, pages 4, 7, 8, 10, 12, 13, 17, 18; © Texas Department of Tourism: cover; © Texas Highways Magazine: pages 15, 21

EDITORIAL SERVICES:
Pamela Schroeder

Library of Congress Cataloging-in-Publication Data

McLeese, Tex, 1950-
    Joining the rodeo / Tex McLeese.
        p. cm. — (Rodeo discovery library)
    Includes index.
    Summary: Describes the events at different levels of rodeo competition, from mutton busting for very young participants to high school and college rodeos and on to the professional level.
    ISBN 1-57103-346-7
    1. Rodeos—Juvenile literature. [1. Rodeos.] I. Title.

GV1834 .M39 2000
791.8'4—dc21

                                            00–022622

TABLE OF CONTENTS

SO YOU WANT TO JOIN THE RODEO?

Lots of children love to play cowboys and cowgirls. Those who love it most might want to join the **rodeo** (ROW dee oh). Rodeo is a sport that uses the riding and **roping** (ROH ping) skills that real cowboys needed in the Old West. This book is about the different levels of rodeo. There are events for children as young as five years old and rodeos for adults, where the champions can earn thousands of dollars. In the rodeo, you can play cowboy for the rest of your life!

Dressed in their rodeo finest.

In the past, rodeo was popular where there were a lot of ranchers. These days, rodeos are held across the country. The sport has fans all across the United States and Canada. Though the cowboy in the Old West is all but gone, rodeo is bigger than ever.

Getting thrown from your horse is a common danger.

MUTTON BUSTERS

Riding bulls and roping calves are too dangerous for the youngest cowboys. Those who want to try rodeo events as young as age five often start by riding sheep. Like bronc or **bareback** (BARE bak) riding, the animal and rider start in a **chute** (SHOOT). When the chute gate opens, the rider tries to stay on the sheep as long as he can. This is called **mutton bustin'** (MUTT un BUS tin), like the **bronco bustin'** (BRON koh BUS tin) of real rodeo.

Learning the ropes.

LITTLE BRITCHES

After **mutton** (MUTT un) bustin', there are rodeos for kids from the ages of 8 to 18. The National Little Britches Rodeo Association runs many of these rodeos. It includes events for both boys and girls. The Junior Rodeo also runs rodeos for kids the same age. In these rodeos, children compete in **calf** (CAF) roping, bareback riding, and other events.

Hands-on rodeo
at a young age.

Trailers for horses can be very costly.

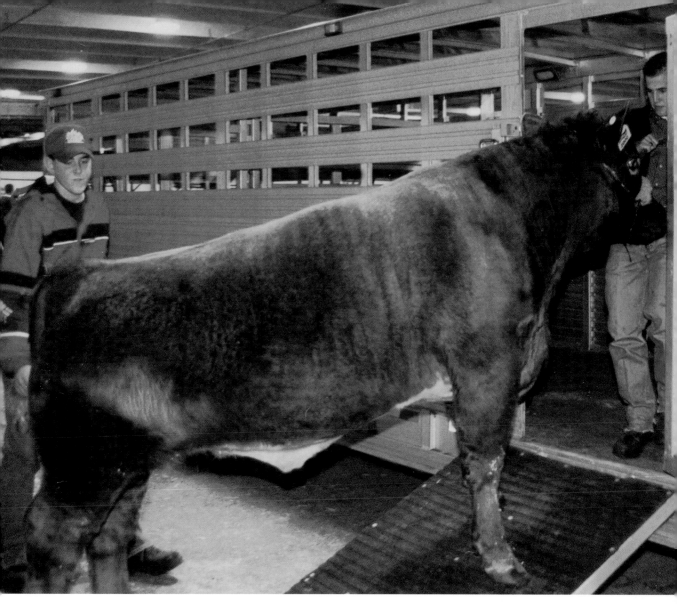

Loading up the steer is another hard job.

HIGH SCHOOL RODEO

Some high schools have rodeo programs just like football or basketball. The National High School Rodeo Association has its High School Rodeo Finals each July. The best rodeo riders between 14 and 18 in the United States and Canada compete. Calf ropers and **barrel racers** (BARE ul RAY serz) own their own horses. That can cost thousands of dollars. It is cheaper to compete in the **roughstock** (RUFF stahk) events such as bull or bareback riding. The rodeo provides the animal.

The rodeo cowboy takes care of his saddle.

COLLEGE RODEO

In the early days of rodeo, few of the cowboys went to college. Today, many in the rodeo compete while going to college. There is a National Intercollegiate Rodeo Association that holds its College National Finals Rodeo every June. The best rodeo riders get "scholarships" that help pay for college, just like the best football or basketball players.

Horses need to have horseshoes.

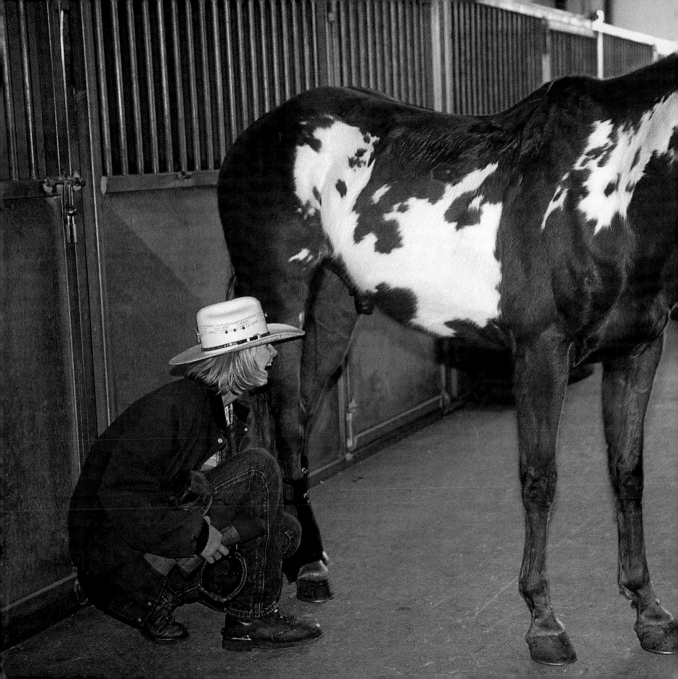

TRAINING SCHOOLS

Many of those who want to ride in rodeos after they've finished high school or college go to rodeo training schools. Those schools have some students who are beginners. Other students are already good enough for professional rodeo but want to get better. The schools last one to four days, and cover everything from fitting equipment to training horses to practice on events.

A skillfull rider enjoys the thrill.

TURNING PRO

A **pro** (PROH), or professional, rodeo cowboy gets money as the prize for winning an event. For many of the pros, rodeo is their full-time job! Many in high school and college rodeo hope to be pros one day, but only the best are able to make their living at it. Rodeo riders need a lot of skill and can be in a lot of danger. Those who are able to stick with the rodeo join the Professional Rodeo Cowboys Association. It holds the National Finals Rodeo every December in Las Vegas.

Man against beast.

THE RODEO LIFE

You have to love the rodeo a lot to want to give your life to it. Rodeo riders don't make as much money as professional baseball or basketball players. However, their sport is a whole lot more dangerous. Every time they try to ride a bucking bull or wrestle a steer, they know they could get hurt. Yet rodeo cowboys wouldn't have it any other way. The danger is part of the thrill. The freedom they enjoy is worth the risk. They get to play cowboy for as long as they want!

GLOSSARY

bareback (BARE bak) — riding without a saddle

barrel racing (BARE ul RAY sing) — a timed event in the rodeo for women on horseback

bronco bustin' (BRON koh BUS tin) — taming wild horses

calf (CAF) — a young cow or bull

chute (SHOOT) — the starting place for riding events

mutton (MUTT un) — meat of a fully grown sheep

mutton bustin' (MUTT un BUS tin) — a rodeo-style event of riding sheep for children

pro (PROH) — short for "professional," doing something for money

rodeo (ROW dee oh) — a sport with events using the roping and riding skills that cowboys needed in the Old West

roping (ROH ping) — catching an animal with a rope

roughstock (RUFF stahk) — one of the rugged rodeo events that is judged on style rather than speed

INDEX